Finding *Love* Again

6 Simple Steps
to a New and Happy Relationship

Terri L. Orbuch, PhD

sourcebooks
casablanca

and misconceptions about relationships makes dating so much easier. By learning what relationship research tells us about how men and women relate, behave, and think, you can approach dating and relationships with fresh, unbiased knowledge. This is important because when you stop buying into the myths, you'll have more realistic expectations. You'll be able to see potential partners for who they really are—rather than who you thought they were going to be. You'll be less frustrated and more likely to find a partner who's a "good fit" for you. And you can stop being swayed by what other people tell you romance is supposed to feel like, or how you've found it to be in your past relationships.

Buying into myths not only affects your attitude and expectations, but also subconsciously drives your behavior. Preprogrammed ideas about love influence how you act on a first date, how you choose to communicate and share ideas with your partner (including how you argue), and how you express feelings of love. Getting rid of these myths from the get-go will boost your odds of dating success, make you more self-aware, increase your confidence and self-esteem, and improve your relationships. Doesn't that sound great?

Where Do Relationship Myths Come From?

Many beliefs about love and relationships have been ingrained in you since your youth. You've picked up impressions and ideas from movies, television, and books. You've been influenced by your family life growing up, how your parents interacted, and by observing the ups and downs in your friends' relationships. And you've probably learned a thing or two about love firsthand. Your former marriage or long-term relationship, and its demise, will always be at the back of your mind—and you may still cringe when you recall those one or two relationships in your life that sizzled and then quickly soured. You may have read self-help books, listened to relationship gurus, gathered advice columns, or replayed tips from popular daytime talk shows. You may have done everything possible to learn about relationships, but the problem is, most of the tips and advice that are out there and repeated as fact are, in actuality, firmly rooted in fiction.

In contrast, the advice and information I'll share with you in this book are based on real, scientific findings—not pop-culture beliefs. And unlike most of the information you will regularly read, hear, or see (which is typically based on unscientific polls or studies with very small groups of people), the findings from my study have been compiled by studying a large group of people over a long period of time. By casting a wide net, my research captures the complex, varied, and common experiences of a diverse group of people. Sure, research studies don't capture everyone's experiences, and the findings can't be applied to each and every person—they are about the average experiences of the average person. But, in most cases, the average experience of the average person can be applied to most of us and our concerns about dating, relationships, and love.

Do You Break the Mold?

As you read the findings from relationship research, don't worry if all of my advice doesn't ring true. About 5 to 10 percent of us "break the mold" in every research study. Some findings will resonate with you in an "aha" moment, *joke and laugh. I asked her to describe her last first date: a blind date with Rick, a guy who works with her best friend. Caitlin's friend was convinced that Caitlin and Rick would hit it off, and this was about all they knew about each other when they met for dinner. Rick was fairly quiet on their date, didn't ask many questions, and selectively told her about his job and interests.*

Caitlin said there was something about Rick that made her instantly feel comfortable. He was warm, good-looking, and smiled a lot. She talked about her mother's recent Alzheimer's diagnosis, told him funny stories about her "evil boss," confessed that she only stays at her job because it's phenomenal money, and even confided about her last relationship and why it didn't work out. Caitlin told me she was on cloud nine by the end of the night. What a fantastic guy! She thought they had really hit it off. Guess what? She never heard from Rick again.

What happened? Caitlin made the same mistake many people do: disclosing too much information on the first date. If you tell all early on—especially intimate and personal information—your date is likely to feel overwhelmed, or worse, he or she may think you tell your life story to everyone. Studies show that people do not want to hear too much, too soon. It's called the "airplane syndrome"—when someone divulges excessive amounts of personal information to a relative stranger. Research has found that these people, who think they're just being honest and open, are viewed by the listener as *not* trustworthy, because they tell all without knowing the other person first.

Airplane Syndrome: Your Pre-Date Safety Check

Picture yourself boarding a plane. You're taking a vacation you've been looking forward to for ages, and in just two short hours, you'll arrive at your destination. You settle into your seat and buckle up, take a deep breath, and relax. Just as you are about to reach for your headphones, your seatmate turns to you and starts to tell you her entire life story: How she had to put in extra time at work to make this trip. How that boss of hers is a complete jerk for not giving her more days off; it's not her fault that she used up all of her vacation days—her allergies were simply off the charts this year! Of course, health issues are the last thing she needs to worry about after the fight she had with her husband about little Johnnie's report card! And with all the fights they've been having lately, she just doesn't feel like being around her husband at all, let alone have sex with him...

You're trapped. You can't escape. You're stuck in your seat on a plane with no way out. By the time the flight ends, you can't get out of there fast enough.

This is exactly how it feels for your date when you disclose too much, too soon, especially on a first date. So before you head out to your next dinner or coffee date with that potential special someone, do your own pre-flight safety check to make sure you keep your life's details in check. Sit down and think about the areas of your life that you wouldn't mind sharing with your date. (This might be work, your family, what you love to do, or the goals you have in life. If you need some ideas, be sure to check out Chapter Five.) Then make a list and check off three to four topics, tops, that you'll actually discuss, and stick to it.

If you want to build trust and be liked by a new partner, disclose personal information gradually over time. If this person is right for you, there will be plenty of time to share personal details. Sharing opinions, stories, history, and other pieces of information bit by bit also makes you more exciting and interesting to a date. It's like eating tiny bites of a heavenly dessert rather than wolfing it all down at once!

When we share personal information with a new date or partner, this process is called *self-disclosure*. Studies show that when the self-disclosure process goes smoothly and both people are comfortable with the process, it creates feelings of deep emotional intimacy or closeness between the two of you. So instead of speeding the process along by revealing too much, focus instead on making the self-disclosure process as smooth as possible.

An Inside Look at Self-Disclosure

What else does research reveal about self-disclosure? Here are some interesting findings to think about:

· **Women typically disclose more than men.** Some men find it difficult to reveal information about themselves and their relationships. If you are a woman dating a man, don't expect your date to tell you quite as much as you may be telling him. If you are a man dating a woman, don't be surprised when she presses you for more information than you care to reveal.

- **Self-disclosure is usually reciprocal.** There is an unspoken understanding in almost every relationship: if one person shares something extremely personal, then the other should respond at the same level of intimacy. Relationship researchers call this the "norm of reciprocity in disclosure." So on the first few dates, if you want the relationship to continue to develop, reveal personal information slowly, so your date won't feel too pressured to respond with his or her personal details. If you find that your date is revealing too much too soon, and you like this person, instead of clamming up, be honest and tell your date: "I appreciate that you're so open with me, but I'm just not as comfortable sharing personal information this soon. Give me a bit more time, though, and I will."

- **Attraction develops and grows with everything you disclose.** Studies show that if you disclose personal information gradually over time, the other person's attraction and positive feelings about you will increase, too. You can also use this information to gauge whether the relationship is going anywhere or getting more serious. If your partner's information becomes more personal as time goes on, it's a clear sign that the relationship is deepening and growing stronger. If your partner is holding back personal information, you may have hit a stumbling block.

Self-disclosure is usually positive—and leads to the other person liking you more or showing support—*unless* your disclosure is too revealing or intimate for the depth of the relationship. If you disclose too much or something that's too personal and your relationship just isn't "there" yet, it may actually produce *dislike*. Since Caitlin and Rick were only on their first date, it's safe to say that one reason the date didn't go well is because Caitlin revealed too much and pushed Rick away.

But there's another reason not to reveal too much before you really know your date: the information you reveal may be viewed *negatively* by the other person. Your date may have a completely different set of romantic beliefs and timetables, different opinions, or may not share the same experiences as you.

So it's not just *how much* Caitlin revealed, but *what* she revealed that may have turned Rick off. For example, Caitlin told Rick that her last boyfriend had spotty employment and income, so she always paid for meals and dates when they went out—which turned out to be one of the reasons they broke up. Now, is it possible that Rick has money issues or feels terrible about his income? Maybe Rick had a past girlfriend who constantly nagged him about not making "enough money," and Caitlin's comment reminded him of that relationship. Caitlin may never know what caused Rick to lose interest, because she revealed *so many things* on their first date.

What has Caitlin learned for her *next* first date? She's learned that her belief in "putting it all out there" is completely off target. Next time, she'll keep the conversation light and funny, which she is very good at, and she won't disclose highly personal information or talk about past boyfriends. A first date should be fun, and not too heavy or serious if you want to go on a second one. Caitlin now realizes that just because she might want to

CHAPTER TWO

Step 2:

Recast Your Past and Start with a Clean Slate

I N THE LAST CHAPTER, you changed your beliefs, reset your expectations, and kicked outdated relationship myths to the curb. You've successfully completed the first step to finding love again.

Next, we'll look at the role *your emotions* play in finding a new partner. This chapter is all about facing your feelings, letting go of the emotional baggage you may be lugging around, and renewing your desire to love again. I'll explain what science shows us about our emotions (and how they can seriously sabotage our relationships), and I'll work with you, step-by-step, with proven strategies that will help you move from the past and into a state where you'll be emotionally available to care for someone again.

It's impossible to leave a serious relationship or go through a divorce without lots of feelings: negative feelings toward your ex, all the hurt and pain from the breakup, missing the contact you had with your in-laws, or feeling worried about your children. You might still be angry at your ex—and you may curse him or her out every chance you get. Or you might still be in shock that the relationship ended, and you catch yourself daydreaming about the good times or secretly wishing you could get back together again. Whether you're "on the market" for a new partner or already seeing someone new, when memories of an old love are triggered by everything from the corner sandwich shop to a favorite song, it can be troubling at best—and destructive at worst.

> ### Emotional Baggage:
> ### Your Love Life in a Suitcase
>
> Do you have strong or painful memories about your past relationships? If you do, you're probably dragging these memories around with you every day, and from relationship to relationship. Emotional baggage is any strong emotion from your past—either negative or positive—that prevents you from being present in your current relationship. Your baggage may be filled with negative emotions ("I can't stand my ex!"), but strong positive emotions or feelings ("She was the love of my life.") add to your baggage, too.

Why It's Important to Work through Your Feelings

Shouldn't you leave the past in the past—and let bygones by bygones? While this may work for small or annoying issues in your life, with relationships, ignoring your feelings will only make matters worse. The relationships we invest in the most, no matter how long we were in them or how long ago they happened, are the ones that have the *biggest* impact on us. And when you still have strong feelings about the past, these emotions can cause all sorts of issues in the present. If you don't work through or tackle these feelings head on, and neutralize your attachment to the past, several things can happen.

You'll miss out on new relationships and experiences. When you hang on to past emotions, you'll always be comparing the past to the present. You may miss out on new experiences and the great things a new partner has to offer, all because you are emotionally handcuffed by what worked, or didn't work, in the past.

You'll become trapped in a cycle of negativity. When you frequently obsess over an old wound, it can wreak havoc on your happiness. My research shows that negative emotions—regardless of their origin—are highly contagious. These emotions are like a giant magnet, pulling and attracting *even more* negativity into your life.

Take, for instance, my client Nick. Nick was still furious with his ex, and he had no problem letting other people know it. Even on dates, Nick would rant about his ex-wife, seething with anger. When his dates avoided him and wouldn't call him back, Nick exclaimed, "I knew it! See, another one didn't call me back! I knew I had a reason to be angry at women."

Even though you may not intend to project the bad feelings you have for your ex onto your date or current relationship, it happens anyway. And when it does, your negative emotions cause other people to view *you* negatively, and eventually, your negativity becomes a self-fulfilling prophecy. Until you work through your unresolved anger or emotions, you may find yourself trapped and unable to move on.

You'll impact your health. By harboring bad feelings and not letting go of the past, you'll bottle up your emotions and increase your chances of becoming physically ill. Research shows that people who don't express emotional pain not only experience greater stress, depression, and anxiety, they also tend to be at an increased risk for other serious illnesses, including heart disease and cancer.

You'll impact your children's well-being. If you have children, conflict or negativity with your ex can affect your children's health, school performance, and overall happiness. Studies show that conflict between parents, and the lack of cooperation after a divorce, significantly lower a child's well-being.

Your Emotions and Your Health

Studies at Southern Methodist University in Texas have shown that people who express their emotions actually improve their immune systems: they have less need to visit their doctors and are healthier overall than their bottled-up counterparts. In another study at Adelphi University in New York, researchers found that people who denied their emotional distress had higher blood pressure than those who could acknowledge their emotional pain and discomfort. Over time, high blood pressure or hypertension, if untreated, can contribute to coronary artery disease and may increase your risk for serious cardiovascular illness.

Now don't misunderstand me. I'm sure you have every reason to feel hurt or angry with your ex. It's also not realistic for me to ask you to stop thinking about the past. But to truly move

Next, you'll want to make an action plan. How can you make these changes happen? For example, if you'd like to get back in touch with your spiritual self, you might join a local church group, commit to a daily meditation, or sign up for an out-of-town spiritual retreat. Want to expand your network of friends? You could volunteer, join a weekend warrior softball league, or invite some buddies over for a Vegas-style poker night. Pick a behavior you honestly can see yourself changing, and develop a plan for the next twenty-one days. Then get busy and stick with it.

Each day, use the chart on pages 92–93 to document your plan *and* your progress. Make note of (1) your actions or behavior, (2) how you feel about the changes that day (do you feel sadness, joy, fear, panic, anxiety?), and (3) any effects, results, or consequences from the change (have other people responded to you, did no one notice, did someone resist your change, was there a strong emotional response?). Write down your thoughts each day as you work on changing your behavior, so you'll remember your *exact* thoughts and feelings, and so you can look back later to see the progress you've made.

By developing this type of action plan, you'll be giving structure and organization to your future. When you're not sure of how to go forward, your plan will remind you of your goals so you can identify the change, act, and move forward. Try an action plan like this for *any* type of change. As long as you can make the commitment to yourself, I promise you'll be surprised at the results.

YOUR 21-DAY ACTION PLAN

What would you like to change in your life? Start by making a goal, then determine what you'll need to do to get there.

For example, if your goal is to work less, you could cut back your working hours, request to work from home one day a week, or take a lunch break out of the office (instead of eating at your desk). Use this calendar each day to document your plan and chart your progress: 1) Record the actions you've taken or the behavior you've changed, 2) Write how you feel about the changes that day, and 3) Note any effects, results, or consequences.

Your personal goal:

_____

Actions or behaviors that will enable you to reach your goal:

_____

DATE	1) ACTION OR BEHAVIOR	2) YOUR FEELINGS OR EMOTIONS	3) RESULTS OR CONSEQUENCES
1.			
2.			
3.			
4.			
5.			
6.			

DATE	1) ACTION OR BEHAVIOR	2) YOUR FEELINGS OR EMOTIONS	3) RESULTS OR CONSEQUENCES
7.			
8.			
9.			
10.			
11.			
12.			
13.			
14.			
15.			
16.			
17.			
18.			
19.			
20.			
21.			

‖ Five Changes That Get Results

In my long-term study, five types of behavioral changes stood out among the rest; men and women who made at least one of these changes were the *most* successful at finding a new partner and a loving, stable relationship. How can you use their secrets to success?

Change #1: Cut your work hours.

Singles who cut their work time by at least one hour a day are more likely to find love. The divorced singles in my EYM study who significantly altered the amount of time they spent at work found new love or remarried at a much higher rate than those who kept their old schedules.

Why does changing your work hours have such an impact on your love life? By cutting your hours, you'll have more time to be out doing something you love—in an environment where you'll be more likely to meet someone with similar interests. By including other activities in your life *besides* work, you'll begin to identify or focus on other aspects of you, which will make you more balanced, whole, and healthy.

Working less, or being able to work "normal" hours, is also an attractive trait to mature daters. Just think: when you work less and explore other things, you'll have a myriad of additional topics and interests to talk about when you meet potential partners. Subconsciously, your date will also know that you have time *for them.*

{ **In my long-term study, five types of behavioral changes stood out among the rest; men and women who made at least one of these changes were the *most* successful at finding a new partner and a loving, stable relationship.** }

Even if you are unable to physically cut back your working hours, you can still make the most of the breaks you have during the day. Take your lunch break out of the office, or take a walk during lunch. You might meet someone, and even if you don't, it will help you take a mental and physical break from work. Or schedule an activity—a weekly class or dinner with a friend—that happens right after work so you'll leave work on time and go straight to the activity at least one day a week.

A break from work was exactly what John, a forty-five-year-old divorced executive from my study, needed. At the urging of some friends, he started to take his lunch breaks out of the office. Here's what he had to say about it:

I work in a busy office, and for years, I've always worked right through lunch. I was having a difficult time meeting new people, so I decided to give "switching up the ol' lunch routine" a try.

I work in a metropolitan area, so there is plenty to do and see at lunchtime. Each day for a few weeks, I ate lunch near one of the outdoor fountains, took a relaxing walk through the park, stopped by a local shop or bookstore, and then headed back to the office.

On one of those walks, it started to storm, so I ducked under an awning—and bumped right into a woman who just happened to be running for cover as well. We got to talking, and I found out that she, too, spent her lunch hour walking through the park and browsing local shops. In fact, she was on her way to my favorite bookstore right before it started to pour! We really hit it off and went on our first date the very next week.

Even if long lunch breaks are out of reach, you may find that you're able to shave off some working time by simply changing how you *think* about time. Researchers at the University of Pennsylvania have discovered that people who constantly think about money or bills fill their time with—you guessed it—work. But when people are made to think about time in general (either *what* they are doing with their time or what they *want* to do with their time) they are more inclined to spend time with the *people* in their lives, and are much happier for it.

When You Get Home, Unplug from Work!

If you work from home, or if you bring the office home with you in the form of voice mail, email, your cell phone, iPhone, Blackberry, laptop, or instant messages, you can effectively change your "working hours" by ditching work distractions while you're at home. It's a great technique for men, but an even more important one if you're a woman.

In one project at the University of Toronto, which studied thousands of men and women in the United States, researchers found that women feel *more guilt and stress than* men when they receive an email, text, or call from work after hours. The men and women in the study were equally effective in balancing work and family, but the ever-present

But eventually, after a slew of dates gone wrong, Martha decided to give in, and she went on a date with Jim, someone her sister had insisted she meet. As Martha tells it, from the moment she and Jim met, there were sparks:

> When Jim and I met, we had an instant connection. I felt like I had known him for years! My sister knew we were both involved in politics, were vegetarians, and had an "off" sense of humor—and wow, was my sister right! Jim and I started out with a handful of dates, and nine months later, there's no breaking us apart. My sister's not one to say "I told you so," so I'll say it for her. She was right! The blind date with Jim was worth it.

Here's why blind dates work: psychologists know that the best choice of a long-term partner is based on the "likes attract" rule—that is, people should seek a partner who is similar to themselves, and one who shares their life values. Guess what? Your friends and family—who know you, love you, and generally want what's best for you—usually set up potential matches for you using the *same* criteria. Blind dates work, whether you're thirty-five or seventy-five, because your friends and family typically select someone they think is similar to you.

Tips to Make Blind Dates Easier

- **Take control.** Don't let others push you into something you don't want to do, and remember you can always say no. You're not obligated to go on a date (or to like someone) just because your mother's boss wants to fix you up with her son. Also, try to be involved: don't let other people set the time and place of the date for you— set it yourself. If you minimize unknown elements of the date as much as possible, you'll create a time, place, and situation that will make *you* feel comfortable.

- **Choose the right place to meet.** A movie is not a good choice for a first date, nor is a loud rock concert. A lunch or dinner date, meeting for a cup of coffee, or even something like miniature golf can make for a great first date. Choose a place where you and your date can talk, observe, and interact.

- **Keep it short.** Whatever activity you choose, keep your date under two hours. A meal is always a good choice for a blind date because it has a beginning, a middle, and an end. When the check comes, your date is over. If it seems too brief, make another date!

- **Don't let the "fixer upper" go on the date with you.** Allowing your matchmaker to join you on your date will create too much pressure and awkwardness; he or she will be watching you and your date like a hawk to see if you've hit it off. If you want to bring your matchmaker along for the initial introduction, that's fine. But agree ahead of time that after ten minutes, he or she will duck out.

- **Chat up the person who introduced you.** Need to get the conversation going? Start by bringing up the person who introduced the two of you. This simple conversation starter gives you both a chance to talk about something other than yourself right away. But be careful about what you say; gossiping can easily come back to bite you.
- **Arrive with an open and positive mind.** Show up with the attitude that this date is an opportunity to meet someone you might not have otherwise met. Even if you don't have romantic chemistry, you may have found a potential friend.

The Third Way to Find New Love: Join an Online Dating Site

Last but certainly not least on the list of top dating strategies is online dating. I'm a huge advocate of online dating, and it's with good reason. Research shows that more than forty million Americans (that's 40 percent of all U.S. singles) turn to the Internet to find the perfect date. About half (51 percent) of all people who meet someone through an online dating service go out on a face-to-face date, and about 20 percent of online daters (over eight million Americans) have turned online dates into a long-term relationship or marriage! Last year alone, *twice* as many marriages occurred for couples who met online than for those who met in bars, clubs, and other social events *combined.* And for homosexual couples, online success rates are even higher: a whopping 61 percent of homosexual couples now in a relationship were the result of an online match.

Did You Know?

Over the past year, the number of people aged fifty and older who use online dating has grown twice as fast as any other age group. And over the past decade, the number of baby boomers who use online dating has more than doubled. According to Match.com, in 2000, 24 percent of baby boomer members visited the dating site each day. In 2010, this number jumped to 69 percent—a growth rate of almost 200 percent!

Over the past ten years, online dating has become a successful way to meet someone who is compatible. Trust me, this isn't by accident. Many online dating services hire psychologists, like me, to assist with how the sites are structured, how online profiles are developed, and how potential dates are matched and recommended to members. In fact, I am the relationship expert for OurTime.com, the largest online dating community catering to singles over fifty years old. As a relationship expert, I answer member questions, help design member surveys, and write articles on dating, love, and relationships for over-fifty men and women who are participating in the online dating experience.

About half (51 percent) of all people who meet someone through an online dating service go out on a face-to-face date, and about 20 percent of online daters (over eight million Americans) have turned online dates into a long-term relationship or marriage.

Between the sheer number of smart dating sites—and the sheer number of people online—online dating has many unique benefits:

- **It's a way to get your feet wet.** Online dating is a great way to "test the waters" and refine what you're looking for in a partner—all before you go out on a date! For example, you may read a profile for "Travel 4 You," a divorced forty-something who loves to explore new and exotic places, and this may make you realize that spontaneous travel tops your wish list for your next relationship. Or you might browse through pages of wild party photos from "Party Girl 73" and decide that a lower-key lifestyle is better suited to you. Online profiles such as these help you to get a better sense of what you want and don't want in a partner. By browsing the site and writing your own online profile—the process of describing yourself and what *you* are looking for—you'll have a better understanding of what you hope to find.
- **You'll avoid feeling shy or nervous.** Type out an online message to someone and then review it, edit it, rewrite it, shorten it, lengthen it—or delete it and start over again. *No one will know.* With an in-person date, you can't take back words once they're out of your mouth. Online, you can practice your repartee before you click "send."
- **You can flirt in your pajamas.** With online dating, you can search for and learn about new people from the comfort of your home, at any hour of the day or night. You're in control of where and when and how. That's empowering!
- **You'll expand the pool of potential partners.** People you meet through regular activities or blind dates tend to fall

within the same circles of friends, family, or acquaintances that already surround you. Online dating opens up a much bigger and broader dating pool, while still affording you total control. You choose the geographic scope for possible suitors, whether it's across town or across the country, and *you* decide who might be right for you.

- **You can cut to the chase, quickly.** With in-person dating, weeks can go by between setting up a date, going on the date, and then waiting to find out if a second date will happen. In contrast, online dating is like the express checkout lane at a convenience store. Between online profiles, emails, conversations, and online chats, you'll quickly find out if someone has the qualities you seek. You can even investigate one, two, five, or ten potential suitors in the same time frame and still have plenty of time for work, volunteering, and dinner with friends.

Online dating easily provides many advantages that would be hard to replicate with other dating methods, even tried and true methods like meeting in a group or going out on a blind date. For many people, online dating rolls the benefits of several dating methods into one, as was the case for Dan, a private client who recently said:

I honestly don't know how I managed to date before. Talking with people online cuts out the time, aggravation, and expense of all of those "first dates gone bad." Now, I'm able to tell if someone might be right for me before we meet in person. And I've been able to meet people who get my dry sense of humor, right off the bat.

This means it could literally be eighteen to thirty-six months before you'll be able to see your partner clearly—strengths, flaws, and all.

That's why you should always take your time when dating. Even if you know who and what you want in a relationship, hold off on running to an Elvis-themed chapel in Vegas to tie the knot as quickly as possible. It's only with time and a more rational perspective that you'll begin to see your partner's full character.

Is It Just Infatuation?

Passionate love, also known as infatuation, can feel like an obsession. During this period, you may feel like a relationship superhero with powers of ultra-focused attention, heightened energy, no need for food or sleep, feelings of euphoria, and unstoppable sexual energy and attraction. You may swear that what you're feeling is love, but you may actually be a victim of your body's hormones instead. Studies have found that the average person experiences infatuation at least six or seven times. Want to put your feelings to the test? Ask yourself the following seven questions:

1. Is your relationship distracting you from work or other responsibilities?

2. Are you having a hard time concentrating and staying focused on anything other than your new partner?

3. Do you constantly feel the need to be together, even if you have to sneak away?

4. Are you ditching activities you enjoyed (or are you neglecting your friends and family) to spend time with your new love instead?

5. Do you ignore or not care what your friends or family think?

6. Have you recently lost weight or find that you just aren't hungry?

7. Do you constantly think about your future, and what your partner thinks about you?

Give yourself one point for each "yes" response, then tally your score. The higher the number, the more likely it is that you are infatuated with your partner, at least for now. My advice? If you have a high score, take your time. You're probably not seeing your partner and the relationship clearly. Don't make any big decisions about your relationship right now.

When you are drawn to someone based *solely* on passion or sexual desire, it may feel like love, but in reality, it's lust—and lust is yet another feeling that's directly influenced by your body's hormones. Scientists have found that the hormone testosterone directly contributes to feelings of lust: the higher the level of active testosterone in a person's bloodstream, the more sexual desire a person experiences, and the more often he or she has sexual thoughts. Can this be confused or misinterpreted as romantic love? Absolutely!

Companionate love, however, develops over time and involves caring and deep emotional intimacy. It stands the test of time even after your body's hormones and love chemicals fade away. In a relationship, you can lust after, be passionate about, *and* love your partner. But studies show that over the long haul, lust and passion aren't the glue that keeps a relationship together. Love is.

Here are a few clues to know if you're experiencing companionate love, rather than feelings of lust or infatuation.

YOU WANT YOUR PARTNER
TO CONNECT WITH YOUR FAMILY.

When you're in love, you are happy when your partner connects with other people in your life—and gets along with the people who are important to you. You want your partner to get a sense of your past, and you like the idea that your family and friends are impressed by this person.

YOU HAVE REALISTIC EXPECTATIONS.

In a loving relationship, you won't be crushed, want to break up, or worry that you'll be dumped whenever you and your partner have a fight. Instead, you'll recognize that conflict is inevitable—it doesn't mean that your partner's feelings have suddenly changed—and you'll find a way to make up.

YOU SPEAK IN "WE," NOT "I."

When two people are in love, their lives are intertwined. By habit, you think of yourself as a "we" or an "us" rather than a "me," "him," or "her." For example, when people ask you what you did this weekend, you might automatically respond by saying, "We went to the movies and had a fantastic dinner," rather than, "I went to the movies with Sandy, and I took her out to dinner afterwards."